A Word of Love

to the Co-workers,

Elders, Lovers, and

Seekers of the Lord

WITNESS LEE

Living Stream Ministry
Anaheim, CA • www.lsm.org

First Edition, January 1999.

ISBN 978-0-7363-0490-0

Published by

Living Stream Ministry
2431 W. La Palma Ave., Anaheim, CA 92801 U.S.A.
P. O. Box 2121, Anaheim, CA 92814 U.S.A.

Printed and bound by CPI Group (UK) Ltd, Croydon, CR0 4YY

09   10   11   12   13   14   /   11   10   9   8   7   6   5   4

CONTENTS

PREFACE

This book is composed of messages given by Brother Witness Lee in Anaheim, California on August 19 through September 16, 1996.

CHAPTER ONE

CORPORATE LIVING
AND THE NEED FOR SHEPHERDING

I thank the Lord that in the last few years, especially since 1991, about two years after we started the full-time training in Anaheim, the Lord has been blessing us in many ways for spreading and for revival. Everything is quite encouraging. The one thing we all have to admit, though, is that we are short of fruit-bearing. This is not only our problem. This has been a problem to all Christians throughout the past two thousand years. If each regenerated believer would bear one fruit yearly, within less than twenty years, <20 yrs the entire world would be saved. However, after almost two thousand years of church history, today's situation related to fruit-bearing is far short of what it should be. Since the end of World War II, the Muslim religion, not Christianity, has been the religion with the most increase. This is a shame to us Christians.

FRUIT-BEARING BEING TO GAIN PEOPLE ONE BY ONE

Fruit-bearing is a big problem. I studied this matter for a long time even before 1984, when I went to Taiwan to study our situation and consider how we should go on. I found out, in principle, that fruit-bearing is not something of a mass movement. It does not take place by great campaigns. Fruit-bearing takes place according to two principles. The first principle is seen in God's creation of man. God created only one man, Adam. Man's multiplication, man's fruit-bearing, is not by mass production but by individual persons bearing children to have a family. At the most, in principle, a family can bear one child a year, twins being an exception. After about six thousand years, the whole earth has been replenished with man. The second principle of fruit-bearing is seen in John 15. Christ is the vine tree and we are His branches to bear fruit. As branches of Christ, according to John 15, our unique responsibility is to bear fruit. Fruit-bearing is by the branches individually. Each branch bears its fruit. This shows us that to have a movement to gain fruit by mass production is wrong. The evangelists in Christianity have big gospel campaigns to convert many people, but where are those people today? Even we have the concept to have big gospel meetings. We may bring several thousand people together to hear the gospel, and take many names, but how many of them do we really gain practically? Our churches remain relatively the same in number year after year. The increase is too slow. I read something which said that a Christian group with an honest pastor who faithfully teaches the Bible and preaches the gospel will gain a yearly increase of ten percent. Do we have this ten percent increase? This shows us that there is a problem with our fruit-bearing.

The problem, I believe, is not with our spiritual life but with our way. Recently, we have seen that John 4:14 reveals the flowing God. God is flowing. In order for a river to flow, there must be a proper way. This is why we must study our way. When I went to Taiwan in 1984, I thought that we should endeavor to baptize many people. In this point we gained a success, but eventually this did not work so well. We had a big gathering in Taipei to gain people through door-knocking. One day we tried to gain three thousand, and we succeeded. Although we gained so many, not many of them are remaining fruit in the church today. We may say that whether they remain in the church or not, they are still saved persons, but this is not practical. Eventually, I found out that the proper fruit-bearing is by individual believers. This is why I started to speak in the United States concerning the vital groups. The vital groups are for fruit-bearing. They are for gaining people one by one.

This earth on which we live is like a great sea full of fish. Since thousands of fish are passing around us day by day, how can we say that we cannot catch one of them within one year?

Is it possible for someone to fish for a year and not catch one fish? Yet for many years this has been the situation among us. Because I have shared concerning the vital groups, we still at least keep the name *vital groups*. Some call themselves "vital groups," but are they vital? Some have had "vital group" meetings for three years, but instead of increasing, they have decreased. Because of this, some have reported to me, saying that door-knocking does not work. This is not true. Two great heretical groups in the United States, the Mormons and the Jehovah's Witnesses, depend almost entirely upon door-knocking. They have nearly no other way for their increase. They only use the one way of door-knocking. According to their statistics of around 1990, the Jehovah's Witnesses in Japan say that they need to knock on six thousand doors to gain one person. However, some of us have only been going out for three weeks or three months without gaining one person and then say that door-knocking does not work. I do not even believe that the Jehovah's Witnesses or Mormons have the best way of door-knocking. According to my study, we have a much better way. I have not spoken enough on the vital groups due to the shortage of time. From this time I will speak on the vital groups for a whole term of the full-time training. Through this speaking we will be able to see that the Lord has shown us a much better way to gain people through door-knocking than that of the Mormons and Jehovah's Witnesses.

CORPORATE LIVING
FOR THE WORK ON THE CAMPUSES

My burden in this message, however, is how to work on the campus and how to have the brothers' and sisters' homes in particular. The brothers' and sisters' homes for corporate living are our invention. Although some in Christianity may have practiced this in the past, I did not learn this from them. I learned this way by our own experience. At a certain time I found that for the campus work we need brothers' homes and sisters' homes. Otherwise, after we catch a "fish," we will have no vessel for keeping it.

At first, it did not seem easy to have the brothers' homes.

This practice started in the church in Taipei, which has practiced having the brothers' and sisters' homes for more than twenty years. They have learned much and experienced much, and now they are enjoying a very big success. According to a recent letter I received, they have one hundred forty new trainees in the current term of the full-time training in Taiwan, most of whom are college graduates from the brothers' and sisters' homes. The goal of those who catch and gain new ones on the campuses is to bring them into the brothers' and sisters' homes. If they cannot bring a saved one into the homes, they feel that this is a failure. In the Orange County area, we have tried to practice the brothers' and sisters' homes. The Lord afforded us some houses through some brothers who love the Lord. The church did not buy those homes, but certain lovers of the Lord bought a number of houses for this purpose. I did not go to see these homes, but word concerning them has come to me.

How to bring people from the campus into the brothers' and sisters' homes is a big problem. We cannot simply tell students that we have a house closer to the school than their dormitory and that it is better for them to stay in our brothers' or sisters' homes. There is nothing wrong with this, but how can we keep them? This is a big problem. Recently in Orange County the number of young people in corporate living has been reducing in number, not increasing. I would like to fellowship with you that you should forget what you have been doing there. Let us learn a new way. To some extent, I do have a new way, which we have learned from the experiences we picked up in Taiwan.

THE PROBLEM OF RECEIVING THE BELIEVERS

Receiving Whom the Lord Has Received

Recently some young people who live in the brothers' and sisters' homes have said that there is a constant demand in corporate living with no supply and no help. This brings us to the principle of receiving the believers, which has been a big problem for nearly two thousand years. Brother Nee spoke with me about the problem of receiving others around 1948

[Handwritten notes at top of page:] We receive ppl as long as Christ has received them. In the church life, we donnot ~~regulate~~ regulate people (waking up. joining ~~this~~ meeting). In the training, yes because we sign up for that. In the church life, we need to receive the Saints even if they don't come to ~~a~~ certain meetings. waking up @ a certain time etc. Love them.

[Handwritten right margin:] shepherd then cherish & nourish them.

when I was with him in Shanghai. This was a great matter in the Brethren practice. The first division among the Brethren was between John Nelson Darby and George Müller over a discrepancy of opinions. Darby said that all the believers who remain in the denominations are companions of evil. He believed that since all the denominations are evil, as long as one joins them, he is a companion of evil. Therefore, he would not receive anyone who still remained in the denominations. George Müller disagreed, pointing out his friend, Hudson Taylor, who was the founder of the China Inland Mission. Müller asked Darby if he could say that Taylor was a companion of evil. This caused the division between the so-called Closed Brethren and Open Brethren. Darby was the first of the Closed Brethren, while Müller was the first of the Open Brethren. The Closed Brethren went too far, even saying that *(1)* if a husband and wife held different opinions, they should not eat together. Recently there has been another big division among the Closed Brethren. One faction says that the believ- *(2)* ers must examine everyone who wants to come to the Lord's table. Before receiving him, they have to study and investigate him. Otherwise, they cannot quickly receive him for the Lord's table. Others, however, say that the believers should simply leave this matter to the Lord and let Him take care of it. These two opinions have existed for many years.

The issue of receiving the believers eventually came to us in China. Brother Nee taught us that according to Romans 14 we have to receive all kinds of different Christians, whether or not they keep certain days and whether they eat meat or vegetables. We should not care for those issues or receive people based upon their keeping of days or their eating. Paul told us that since the Lord has received them, we also have to receive them. The Southern Baptists, however, do not receive someone unless he is baptized by them, not only by immersion but by their pastor and in their water. They are very strict and do not recognize any other kind of baptism. Baptism by immersion by their pastor and in their water is the requirement of the Southern Baptists for receiving people into their church life.

When we practiced the church life according to Brother

Nee's teaching and according to the Bible, we also faced these problems. Therefore, when I came to this country in 1960, I spontaneously impressed the brothers that we must keep the Lord's table open. I realized that, especially in the United States, there are many believers who are not only saved and regenerated but who also love the Lord, and they are tired and disgusted with the practice of investigating a person about so many matters. I felt that we should not take this way. We have the Lord's table, and whosoever will may attend. Even today it is still the same with us.

Depending on God's Selection

According to history, the children of many nominal Christians become real Christians. I was one of these children. My mother was not saved; she was merely nominal, but when she was young, she stayed with her grandfather who was a good Southern Baptist, and he sent her to study at a Southern Baptist school. Because of this, she was one hundred percent for Christianity. In our home she taught us stories from the Gospels. She had printed tracts pasted on the wall. That was very unusual in our country. When we were growing up, she wanted us to go to her church. She washed our clothes for us on the Lord's Day, she prepared better meals on that day, and she brought us to her church. She was not saved, yet my second sister got saved, then I, and then my younger brother. Three of her children were not only saved but also became seeking Christians.

I have seen many devoted Christians. Among them, one was Brother Nee. Not all of Brother Nee's brothers were properly saved. Brother Nee's mother was a sister who loved the Lord very much. It is no wonder that she would weep for her sons. I have seen many others like this. Even among us there are many good sisters who love the Lord very much and pray for their children nearly every day, even though their children do not believe. On the other hand, some parents are not so devoted, yet their children love the Lord. Eventually, I have bowed down before the Lord. The Lord's word is true. We should raise up our children according to the Lord's teaching. This is our duty and we should do it, but eventually their salvation and seeking of the Lord depend upon God's eternal choosing and predestination. If our raising of our children could decide their spiritual future, this would be against God's predestination.

Isaac brought forth two sons as twins. One was Esau and the other was Jacob. The Bible says clearly in Malachi 1:2-3, "I loved Jacob; but Esau I hated." This creates a very big problem in theology. For this reason there is Calvinist theology and Arminian theology. The former says that our salvation is up to God's choosing, and the latter says that our salvation is our responsibility and according to our endeavoring. The Arminians say that we can be saved in the morning and lost in the evening. The Pentecostals are Arminians, while the Presbyterians are Calvinists. The Lutherans also teach that salvation is not up to us. Whether we go to the theater or whatever we do, as long as we have been chosen, our eternal security is fixed because it depends upon God's choosing. One day a student came to D. L. Moody, the American evangelist who founded the Moody Bible Institute, saying, "I dare not to go out to get people saved because I am afraid that someone may be saved whom God did not choose." Moody answered, "On the outside lintel above the gate into heaven it is written, 'Whosoever will may come,' but on the inside it says, 'Chosen before the foundation of the world.'" It is difficult to say who is chosen. We simply must do our duty to raise up our children according to the teaching of the Lord. Whether or not they have been chosen is not up to us. Some may say, "Because it is not up to us, we need not do much." However, this also is wrong.

THE PROBLEM OF REGULATIONS
IN CORPORATE LIVING

Not Exercising Demands through Regulations

According to my observation in Taipei, it is better not to exercise any demand on the young people who live in our brothers' and sisters' homes. We have to realize that the arrangement of these homes is to bring people to the Lord and to gain them, just as the Lord came to seek the lost sheep.

The Lord comes to seek the lost sheep, not the good sheep. Therefore, the brothers' and sisters' homes should have no regulations. To save sinners we also should not have regulations. As long as we have regulations, we regulate people away. We thank the Lord that we have the brothers' and sisters' homes as "fishing hooks," and some young people have been hooked. It is not so easy for us to hook a person, so if we have regulations, they will keep people away. The brothers' and sisters' homes may have a regulation that says everyone must return home and turn off their lights by 10:00 P.M., but some young ones may be excluded by this regulation. What shall we do? Should we have no regulation about the time to sleep? We should have a proper kind of regulation, but we should make it clear to the young ones that this kind of regulation is to help them to have a proper physical life. We hope that they would keep the proper regulation, but it is not something legal. In the brothers' and sisters' homes, nothing should be legal. There should be freedom, not legality.

Some may ask, "If the young people do not return before 10:00 P.M., what shall we do?" For this, we need shepherding. According to the principle in Ephesians 5, the Lord shepherds us by cherishing us and nourishing us (v. 29). We have to shepherd the young ones by cherishing and nourishing them. This requires that we spend time with them. The co-workers may not have much time, but they should train some students who live in our brothers' and sisters' homes, so that two or three will become their helpers. They have to carry out the shepherding with love. Do not condemn the young ones. Do not say, "Since you have broken the rule, you cannot stay here" and simply look on as they leave. We have to shepherd them.

The Danger in Disciplining Young Ones

All parents know that every child is naughty. Some babies throw their rice bowl when their mother is feeding them. What should the mother do? The mother mostly cherishes them to make them happy, and by cherishing them, she feeds them. Parents raise their children by cherishing them in many ways. I have eight children; I have suffered much, and

I have learned all the lessons. Ephesians 6:4 says, "Fathers, do not provoke your children to anger, but nurture them in the discipline and admonition of the Lord." When we discipline our children with provoking, our discipline is of no value. If we are going to discipline a child, we must go to the Lord and say, "Lord, take away my provocation." This is very hard. Some parents whom I have taught in this way have said that without being provoked they cannot discipline their child. To them, punishing a child requires that they be provoked. Parents must remember not to spank their child when they are provoked. If one is offended by his child, he becomes a provocation to him, and he loses his capacity to discipline the child. When one is angry, he should not touch his children. He should leave them, kneel down, and pray. Then, when he is cherished by the Lord, he can go back to his children to cherish them. We need cherishing. When a parent provokes his child and spanks him, the child may leave home and run away. Then the parent needs to spend time to find him and bring him back. Many children after being provoked to anger and spanked leave home and do not want to come back. Eventually, the parent has to submit to them, bowing down his head to beg them to come back home, and he may have to gain them back indirectly through a big brother, a cousin, or some other relative.

Luke 15 first tells us how the Lord as the Shepherd sought for the one lost sheep. Second, the woman, signifying the Holy Spirit, lit a lamp and searched the house to find the lost coin. Third, a father lost his son, the prodigal, who eventually returned. The son prepared an apology for his father, but the father was already waiting to receive him. The son did not first see the father; the father first saw him and ran to him. The Brethren teacher from England under whom I first learned this chapter taught us that in the entire Bible only Luke 15 says that God ran. God only ran once, and it was to receive a returning prodigal son. In Brother Nee's preaching concerning the loving father who watched for his son's return, he once told a story of a naughty boy who ran away after being punished by his father. The father sat in his living room every night for many days expecting to receive

his son back. One night the naughty boy came back home and
was surprised to see his father still sitting there. The father
said, "Son, since you left I have been sitting here every night
waiting and expecting to receive you back." This is a father's
heart. Our brothers' and sisters' homes should be like this,
full of love and full of expectation.

Gaining People through a Proper Spirit

One day Hall Three in the church in Taipei had a time
with all the parents of the ones who lived in the brothers' and
sisters' homes. The brothers showed all the parents their
children's living room, dining room, dormitory, and beds.
Many parents were inspired by this. They went out to tell
other parents to send their children to certain schools close to
those homes. Some of the unsaved parents were even saved
because of that demonstration. We should have this kind of
spirit. If we have this kind of spirit, the number of houses
that we now have will not be sufficient. The more houses we
have, the better it will be. This is one of the ways for us to
bear fruit. The brothers in Taipei have the assurance that
they can gain people in this way.

When school opens, the brothers and sisters also go to the
campus to set up a table and get the names of the freshmen.
Then the brothers and sisters work on those persons. In a
similar way, the Mormons in the United States teach their
young people to speak good Mandarin and send them to the
airport in proper attire. They stand at the entry and watch
the new young people come in. They greet them in Mandarin
and ask if they are students coming to attend school. Then
they take their address and offer them a ride. This is the
way they gain people.

Studying and Categorizing the Young Ones

We must have a clear view about the way we practice
the brothers' and sisters' homes. For the homes we should
keep the principle that we are a loving people. We are trying
to gain people, to bear fruit. Therefore, we should not regulate the brothers and sisters. We must study the way we
take in the homes. In education there are at least six levels:

kindergarten, elementary school, middle or junior high school, high school, college, and graduate school. We treat these six kinds of students in six different ways. What we exercise over the high schoolers, we should not exercise over the kindergarten students. If we do, we may kill them. Likewise, what we practice with the kindergarten students, we should not practice with the elementary students. We have to change our way or we will spoil them.

No child under six likes to play mainly with adults. They prefer to play with others who are under six. Even on the campus, those who labor there should not be too old. If they are too old, no one will come to them. The students may run away because they are afraid of older people. A young man may feel uncomfortable with old men, but when someone his own age comes, he is happy. This illustrates that we cannot have the same regulation for people of different ages. We must classify people. We should have some homes for those in their first year, and gradually we can advance from there up to the fourth year. Those who have stayed with us for several years have been growing in the Lord, and they can now live a corporate life. In order to prevent some from feeling superior or inferior when we classify them, we must do it wisely. When parents raise their children, they exercise a certain way with each one. To open up a kindergarten is not easy. The government has many regulations for nurseries and kindergartens. A nursery, for example, must care for the children's health and avoid contagious diseases. We should not take a simple way. We cannot avoid a feeling of superiority among the young people, just as the students in high school feel superior about being in high school. Therefore, we need spirituality. We have to teach them to deny the self and many other matters. This is not easy, and it requires much study. I would ask the brothers who set up the homes for the brothers and sisters to please reconsider the way we take. We cannot do things in a simple way. Educators know the psychology of students; they know the difference between kindergarten, elementary, junior high, high school, college, and graduate school. We must be careful in these matters.

OUR NEED FOR FURTHER TRAINING AND LEARNING

I expect that I could have a further time with the elders to train them how to behave as elders. I take care of two annual trainings, and formerly I had to write thirty messages for thirty meetings. I also needed to travel much abroad, and recently I became ill due to traveling. Therefore, since I came to this country, I did not have much time to sit down with the elders to speak in this way. The brothers who are elders in the United States are probing for the way to be good elders, but they do not know what to do. Not one of us was born knowing everything. Therefore, we need to learn, practice, and be educated. Even the two-year full-time training makes a big difference, but so many elders have not been trained. I spoke of some of these things in *The Elders' Management of the Church,* but I did not have the time to look into all these matters very much. I now question whether *management* was the right word to use in that book. Our use of this word was also due to my lack of time to look into all these matters. What does "the elders' management" mean? The church is not a bank or a corporation that needs a manager. For practical reasons, we have a manager in the Living Stream Ministry office, but there is no rank in this office.

We need very much fellowship so we can learn. There is much profit for brothers from one part of the country to visit another, not to teach or merely to learn but simply to observe. Likewise, it is a big help to travel to another country and stay there for some time. In this way we can learn much. I have been traveling throughout the whole world, and I have learned much. I truly learned something from the Japanese, and I learned something further from the Koreans. We should never merely be natives of our own country. We should try to go out and learn.

THE NEED FOR SHEPHERDING,
ESPECIALLY BY CHERISHING

To me, shepherding means everything for the brothers' and sisters' homes, for the vital groups, for the church, and for the elders. In Christian teaching, nearly no one stresses this matter, but it is a great matter. The Lord is not only our

Shepherd and Overseer outwardly; He is also the Shepherd and Overseer of our souls (1 Pet. 2:25). I have stressed this in the *Crystallization-study of the Gospel of John.*

Today in the United States it is very hard to teach school. Even professors have to study how to shepherd their students. If they do not shepherd them, they may have serious problems. The first point of shepherding is cherishing. Ephesians 5 tells us that the Lord cherishes and nourishes the church, His Body. Without cherishing, nourishing by itself does not work. Today I handle things and do things very differently from the way I did thirty years ago. Within these thirty years I have learned much, even related to dealing with my children. We are touching society, and we are touching human beings. This is not a simple matter, so we must learn.

We may do the work of the ministry, but the unfitting manner in which we behave and conduct ourselves kills our ministry. Recently, a graduate student in a certain university attacked his three professors because they would not pass him. We cannot say that these professors were not responsible in part for this. If they had spoken softly and wisely, their student would not have been provoked to such an extent. Those professors were trying their best to help this student, but the result was the opposite. Many other professors who heard of this tragedy will now learn to be careful in dealing with students. In principle, it is the same with us. The result, the issue, of our work very much depends on our way of conducting ourselves. We are taking care of the brothers' and sisters' homes, but how do we conduct ourselves, how do we behave, and what way do we take? Even in caring for our children, if we are angry, we will provoke them. We must not do that. Ephesians is a very high book, but it comes down to say, "Be angry, yet do not sin; do not let the sun go down on your indignation" (4:26). If we had written Ephesians, we may not have added this word. We may have spoken only the high peaks in the first three and a half chapters of this book, but Paul came down from the high peaks in the second half of chapter four and chapters five and six. These portions are very meaningful. Similarly, James says, "The wrath of man does not accomplish the righteousness of God" (1:20).

John 10 and 21 are chapters on shepherding. Chapter ten speaks of the Lord's coming as the Shepherd. He is the Shepherd, and He is the door in and the door out to the pasture. In 10:10 He says, "I have come that they may have life and may have it abundantly," and in verse 11 He says, "I am the good Shepherd." He also says that He lays down His human life for the sake of shepherding. To give life requires shepherding. Without shepherding, it is hard for the divine life to work within us. Chapter twenty-one is a very important appendix on shepherding. John is a book on the divine life, but the divine life depends upon shepherding. Even in our human life, family life, and marriage life there is the need of shepherding, and shepherding requires cherishing. Husbands and wives need to cherish each other all the time. If a couple does not know how to cherish each other, they will have trouble. Parents also need to shepherd their children. If shepherding could be practiced everywhere, the whole of society would become a utopia. Misunderstandings and oppositions mainly come from the shortage of shepherding. We the co-workers must learn to cherish people.

Our roommate is the one who should cherish.

One-on-One shepherding starts from the ppl around us.

CHAPTER TWO

SHEPHERDING PEOPLE
ACCORDING TO THE LORD'S HEART

Scripture Reading: John 3:16; 1 Tim. 1:15; 1 John 4:10; Matt. 9:10-13; Luke 7:34-50; 15:1-24; James 5:19-20; Prov. 10:12; Gal. 6:1-2

In this message we will fellowship concerning how we should learn of the Lord to shepherd people according to His heart. This fellowship is not merely a teaching, instruction, or rebuke; it is a shepherding to us.

LOVE COVERING ALL TRANSGRESSIONS

The way that some of you have spoken concerning corporate living has bothered me. Proverbs 10:12 says, "Hatred stirs up strife, / But love covers all transgressions." If we hate each other, we will have endless strife, but love covers not only one sin or some sins, but all sins. James ends his writing by saying, "My brothers, if any one among you is led astray from the truth and someone turns him back, let him know that he who turns a sinner back from the error of his way will save that one's soul from death and will cover a multitude of sins" (5:19-20). Should we hate one who is not up to the standard, who is led astray from the truth, or should we love him? We may not love those who are not able to live in corporate living. We may only love the particular group of those who live properly in our homes. This is altogether not according to the Spirit of the Lord as revealed in the Bible. If a brother is good, he does not need our love very much because he has already been sufficiently loved. Nearly everyone loves a good person, but what about one who is led astray from the truth? If a brother is led astray from the truth to attend the

denominations or go to the movies, our small group may feel
that we do not need him, and we do not accept him because he
is not qualified. This is not love; this is hate. Love covers
many sins. Even if we know that he goes to the movies, we
should not tell others. This is to cover him. We do not like to
uncover him or expose him. To uncover is not love. Hatred
stirs up strife, but love covers all sins. We would rather be
like the sons of Noah who covered their father's nakedness
which was due to his drunkenness. We do not like to uncover
others. Covering brings in blessing, but uncovering brings in
a curse. This is not a small matter. Those who uncover suffer
the curse, but those who cover others' sins, defects, and
shortcomings enjoy, gain, and receive blessing. "Cover a multitude of sins" in James 5:20 is an Old Testament expression
used by James to indicate that turning an erring brother back
is to cover his sins so that he is not condemned. *Cover...sins*
here equals *sins...forgiven* in verse 15, as in Psalm 32:1,
which says, "Blessed is he whose transgression is forgiven; /
Whose sin is covered." It is the same in Psalm 85:2.

GOD LOVING THE WORLD
FOR SINNERS TO HAVE ETERNAL LIFE,
THAT IS, TO BECOME THE NEW JERUSALEM

By reading all the above verses, we can see the heart of
our God and of our Savior Jesus Christ. John 3:16 says, "For
God so loved the world that He gave His only begotten Son,
that every one who believes into Him would not perish, but
would have eternal life." The heart of our God is to love not
only righteous men but sinners, even the world, which is
worse than mere sinners. *World* denotes the sinful, fallen
people. The entire human race became the world, just as the
entire divine race, the new race, will become the New Jerusalem. The New Jerusalem is the totality, the consummation, of
the eternal life, while the world is the totality, the consummation, of the fallen race. It is a hardship for translators to
translate verse 16. The Chinese version renders it in a way
that can be interpreted, "God loved the people on this earth."
This is inadequate. The world denoting the fallen race is seen
in the word *flesh* in Genesis 6:3, which says, "My Spirit shall

not always strive with man, for that he also is flesh." Because all the people on this earth became flesh, God decided to temporarily forsake the world, which He loved, for a purpose. God loved the fallen human race, who became so rotten as to be one with Satan. The *world* indicates man becoming one with Satan, becoming Satan's cosmos, the satanic system that systematizes all people. In this way, *world* is worse than *sinners* because it denotes that man is incorporated with Satan. *World,* denoting the human race in John 3:16, is a very bad term. God so loved the world, sinful people in their worst denotation, that He gave His only begotten Son, not so that they would go to heaven but that whoever believes into Him would not perish but have eternal life.

John 3:16 is a new verse to us. We generally interpret this verse to mean that if we believe in the Lord Jesus as the Son given by God, we will have His divine life. That is right, and there is nothing wrong with this, but the goal of having the divine life is the New Jerusalem. God loved the human race, the worst human people, with the intention that they all may participate in the New Jerusalem. Eternal life here is the same as in 4:14, which says, "The water that I will give him will become in him a spring of water gushing up into eternal life." To have eternal life means to be joined to, to participate in, the New Jerusalem. The banners for the *Crystallization-study of the Gospel of John* say that the Triune God who passed through all the processes, the all-inclusive Christ who was incarnated to die and resurrect, and the life-giving Spirit who was consummated to indwell us all take the New Jerusalem as Their eternal goal. When I wrote this utterance, I realized that few would understand why I used it for a crystallization-study of John, but it is the conclusion of my study of John. In this crystallization-study I thoroughly and intrinsically came to the clear conclusion that this Gospel, especially from chapter one to chapter four, is the record of the flowing God in His three stages: the Father as the fountain, the Son as the spring, and the Spirit as the flowing river. Moreover, They all take the New Jerusalem as Their eternal goal. Apparently, the New Jerusalem is not mentioned in John. However, it is seen in the eternal life in

4:14. *Eternal life* here is the totality of the divine life. A man
is the totality of the human life; each one of us is the totality
of the human life, but the divine life has only one totality in
the whole universe—the New Jerusalem.

The Bible teaches us that eternal life is God Himself. In
the beginning there is God as the eternal life, and the consummation of God as the eternal life is the New Jerusalem.
The Bible consummates in the New Jerusalem, which is the
very God who was in the beginning. How does God become
the New Jerusalem? It is through His flowing. The Bible has
two ends, Genesis 1—2 and Revelation 21—22. At the beginning of the Bible there is God, at the end there is the New
Jerusalem, and in between are hundreds of pages speaking
about all the matters related to the eternal life, including the
believers, regeneration, transformation, conformation, and
glorification. This is the proper way to view the Bible. All the
activities of the eternal life take the New Jerusalem as the
final goal. This is the meaning of "into eternal life" in John
4:14. The word *into* is also used in 1 Corinthians 12:13, which
says that the Gentiles and the Jews have all been baptized in
one Spirit into one Body. *Into one Body* does not mean merely
to enter into the Body but to become the Body. In the same
way, *into eternal life* does not merely mean to enter into the
New Jerusalem as the eternal life but to become the New
Jerusalem as the eternal life. The coming New Jerusalem
will be you and me. We are the New Jerusalem. The New
Jerusalem is still under a consummating work, and this
consummating work is the flow of the divine life. This is very
deep.

**THE LORD NOT COMING
TO CALL THE RIGHTEOUS BUT SINNERS**

First Timothy 1:15 says, "Faithful is the word and worthy
of all acceptance, that Christ Jesus came into the world to
save sinners, of whom I am foremost." Christ Jesus came into
the world, which, as we have seen, is not a positive term. He
came into the world, into the fallen human race, to save
sinners. Paul, as Saul of Tarsus, was the top sinner. If Christ
came only to save gentlemen, to save righteous men, Paul

would have been finished. He could not have participated in God's salvation. In coming to save sinners, Christ took the sinners as His object. His heart is to save us, the sinners in the world.

First John 4:10 says, "Herein is love, not that we have loved God but that He loved us and sent His Son as a propitiation for our sins." We may never have been impressed with the intrinsic significance of verses like this. God is love; it is not that we loved God, but that He loved us. We never cared for God, and we forsook Him. *Us* in this verse refers to the world. God not only loved the world, but He also loved us. Moreover, His love is shown in that He sent His Son as a propitiation for our sins.

Matthew 9:10-13 says, "As He was reclining at table in the house, behold, many tax collectors and sinners came and reclined together with Jesus and His disciples. And when the Pharisees saw it, they said to His disciples, Why does your Teacher eat with the tax collectors and sinners? Now when He heard this, He said, Those who are strong have no need of a physician, but those who are ill. But go and learn what this means, 'I desire mercy and not sacrifice,' for I did not come to call the righteous, but sinners." The house mentioned here is not a corporate-living house; it is a house of sinners and tax collectors. Jesus, though He was the God-man, feasted there with them, reclining at the table. He enjoyed that time, and all the tax collectors and sinners, the ancient "gangsters," joined together with Him. That offended the Pharisees. The Pharisees here may be compared to the ones who regulate the corporate living homes. The "corporate-living Pharisees" came and asked why Jesus was eating with the "gangsters" and "bank robbers." The Lord answered that those who are strong have no need of a physician. If one is healthy enough to live properly in corporate living, he does not need a vital group as a "health clinic." A strong, healthy man does not need to go to a clinic. Jesus, the Son of God, did not come for the strong men; they do not need Him. He came for the ill ones. The vital groups are set up not for those who are healthy and strong and able to live in corporate living, but for those who return to the brothers' homes after midnight. God desires mercy, not sacrifice. If we sacrifice and offer much to Him without mercy, He does not like it. First Corinthians 13:3 says, "If I dole out all my possessions to feed others, and if I deliver up my body that I may boast, but do not have love, I profit nothing." To give everything for others without love means nothing. Mercy is the usher of love. To love those who are poor requires that we have mercy on them. The Lord did not come to call the righteous but the sinners. This is His heart.

HAVING A SPIRIT TO GO
TO TAX COLLECTORS AND SINNERS

Luke 7:34-50 also speaks of the Lord Jesus being with sinners and tax collectors. Verse 34 says, "The Son of Man has come eating and drinking, and you say, Behold, a gluttonous man and a drunkard, a friend of tax collectors and sinners." If we see one who is a drunkard drinking beer, we certainly would stay away from him. We would rather go to one who is a saint living properly in corporate living. This kind of spirit now is spreading everywhere around the globe in the Lord's recovery. We love those in the proper corporate living, but we do not love the ones who go to the movies or drink beer. Instead, we may gossip about them. This is the spirit that fills all the churches. Some may charge me, saying, "Did you not teach us concerning beer drinking?" Yes, I have taught about this, but there is another side. Believe me, in the New Jerusalem no one will drink beer again. At that time, the beer drinkers will all be in the lake of fire. But today Christ is the heavenly ladder. He is not a flat stairway but a standing stairway. Previously, we were in "hell." When I was under twenty, I played mah-jongg behind my mother's back; all the Chinese like to play mah-jongg, but one day a heavenly ladder appeared to me, and I climbed it. I left the mah-jongg table and climbed to the New Jerusalem.

I can never forget a certain pastor. While I was playing mah-jongg, he came to me every week. My older sister was studying in the highest women's seminary in China. She loved the Lord at that time, and she knew I was not gained by the Lord, so she committed me to this pastor. After that commitment, he came to me every week for about three or four months, but he did not speak much. Finally, at the end of December he said, "Mr. Lee, you are busy at the end of the year because in your business you have many things to do. Therefore, I will not come to you next week. I will wait until the New Year is over." He did not come, but remarkably, the heavenly ladder came. As all the Chinese know, the second day of the Chinese New Year is a day of rottenness, gambling, and all manner of entertainment. On that day, I rose and put on my best, new clothes. After breakfast, as I stood there in my new clothes, my mother asked me, "What shall you do today?" As I considered her question, I could not speak. Right away without thinking I said, "I shall go to Pastor Yu's church." My mother was very happy. Then I went to that denominational church. That was my first time to climb the heavenly ladder. Christ went to a house full of sinners and tax collectors. The vital groups, the co-workers, and the elders should pick up this spirit, the spirit of God loving the world, the spirit of Christ coming to the worst homes in order to gain people and put them upon Him as the heavenly ladder that they may ascend on Him.

HAVING THE LOVING AND FORGIVING HEART OF OUR FATHER GOD AND THE SHEPHERDING AND SEEKING SPIRIT OF OUR SAVIOR CHRIST

I love Luke 15. Verse 1 says, "Now all the tax collectors and sinners were drawing near to Him to hear Him." The gentlemen and righteous men were not joined to Him, but the tax collectors and sinners were. Therefore, the Pharisees murmured and complained again. Then the Lord spoke three parables. The first is concerning a shepherd seeking the one, unique, lost sheep. Of one hundred, this one was a lost one, so the shepherd came purposely for him. Why did the Lord go to a house full of sinners and tax collectors? It was because among them there was one lost sheep of His, whom He had come to seek. The second parable is concerning a woman who lit a lamp and swept the house to seek her lost coin. The third parable is about the prodigal son. The shepherd is the Son,

the woman is the Spirit, and in the parable of the prodigal
son there is the Father. As the prodigal son was returning,
he was preparing and considering what to speak to his
father. He prepared himself to say, "Father, I have sinned
against heaven and before you. I am no longer worthy to be
called your son; make me like one of your hired servants"
(vv. 18-19). While he was walking and thinking like this, the
father saw him. Verse 20 says, "But while he was still a long
way off, his father saw him and was moved with compassion,
and he ran and fell on his neck and kissed him affectionately."
That the father saw the son a long way off was not an acci-
dent. From the time the son left home, the father must have
gone out to look and wait for his coming back every day. We do
not know how many days he watched and waited. When the
father saw him, he ran to him. This is the Father's heart. The
father interrupted the son while he was speaking his prepared word. The son wanted to speak the word he had
prepared, but the father told his servants to bring the robe,
the ring, and the sandals and to prepare the fattened calf. A
teacher among the Brethren told me that in the whole Bible
we can see God run only one time, in Luke 15, where the
father sees the returning prodigal son. He ran; he could not
wait. This is the Father's heart.

To speak truthfully, we have lost this spirit among the
co-workers, elders, and vital groups. We do not have such
a loving spirit that loves the world, the worst people. We
classify people, choosing who are the good ones. Throughout
my years I have seen many good ones. Eventually, very few of
the good ones remain in the Lord's recovery. Rather, so many
bad ones remain. In the beginning I also was one who
classified them as bad, but today many bad ones are still
here. If it were according to our concept, where would God's
choosing be? Our choosing depends upon God, who chose His
people before the foundation of the world. The Bible says that
God hated Esau and loved Jacob. If we were there, none of us
would have selected Jacob. This man was too bad. We would
have selected Esau, the gentleman. From his mother's womb,
Jacob was fighting, and when he was born, he grabbed his
brother's heel. Eventually, he did everything that caused

Esau to want to kill him. His mother Rebecca knew this, so
she sent him away to his uncle's house, but when he went
there, he did the same thing; he cheated his uncle by getting
four wives from him. This is to live like a gangster. None of us
would have chosen Jacob. It is not up to our choosing, our
selection. It is based upon God's eternal selection.

Do not classify people. Who can tell what they will be?
When I was playing mah-jongg at the age of eighteen or
nineteen, who would have thought that this mah-jongg player
would sit in America many years later to talk to people about
the Lord? Who brought me here? It was Christ as the
heavenly ladder. He brought me up to God in the heavens,
and He brought me down to the earth with Himself. The
heavenly ladder has many steps, and God brought me up not
in one year but over many years. When I arrived at the top, I
met God, and He equipped me and sent me back down. I came
down, first to Taiwan, then to the South Asian islands, and
then to this country. Now I am here. The pastor in my
hometown did not say of me, "I know this man. He is a
gambler, a mah-jongg player. I do not like him, and I do not
want to have such a member in my church." Rather, he visited
me, and one day very mysteriously the seeking Spirit was
seeking in me, like the woman in Luke 15.

Why would I spend so much time on this subject? I want
to shepherd and disciple you from the Bible so you can see
this matter and have a change. I am discipling you to change
your concept. The God-man concept is that Christ came to
save sinners, especially the top sinners. He saves the
"gangsters," even the leader of the "gangsters," Saul of
Tarsus. Paul said, "Faithful is the word and worthy of all
acceptance, that Christ Jesus came into the world to save
sinners, of whom I am foremost" (1 Tim. 1:15). Paul could say
this because he was the top sinner opposing Christ. He
rebelled against Christ, but while he was rebelling, Christ
knocked him down, called him, and saved him. Jesus Himself
said, "Those who are strong have no need of a physician, but
those who are ill....I did not come to call the righteous, but
sinners" (Matt. 9:12-13). That is why He was there among the

sinners and tax collectors, eating and feasting with them, reclining at the table and enjoying with them.

If we lose this spirit, whether we are elders, co-workers, or serving ones, we are finished. This is the main reason why we are so barren, bearing no fruit for so many years. Recently a brother went to care for a couple, but he did not have this spirit. He visited them no more than ten times and became disappointed. Since the couple had no heart for this brother, he reported that it was useless to visit them further. When Pastor Yu visited me, I did not care for him, but he continued to come for three or four months, week after week. We need to have this spirit. We all have to change our concept. Therefore, we need discipling. We have too much of the natural thought. We need to be discipled to have the divine concept, the concept of the Father's heart and the heart of the Lord Jesus, who came to save sinners.

Do not say that your vital group is only for those in corporate living, and do not label people. We like to rank people, saying that the co-workers are the first rank, while others are the subsequent ranks. This is absolutely wrong. There is no rank. We all are the people in the world and in the flesh. Even today I am very wary that I may do something by my flesh. If I am not wary, I will still live by my old life. When I talk to my wife, I have to be careful; otherwise, I will talk to her in the natural life. Then I will have to confess, "Lord, even in the matter of the way I talked to my wife I was not conformed to Your death. I did not do it in Your resurrection." Dear saints, are these things merely teachings to us? As the final item of the way to overcome the degradation of the church, 2 Timothy 4:22 says, "The Lord be with your spirit. Grace be with you." This refers to the Lord Jesus as the life-giving Spirit in our spirit to be the abiding grace. He is abiding, remaining, in our spirit all the time as grace for our enjoyment. However, I have checked with myself, saying, "Do you live such a life? Every day, every moment, do you enjoy the Lord Jesus as the Spirit in your spirit to be the abiding grace?" I have to admit that I do not. The Lord knows that every morning I pray, "Lord, thank You for another day. I am still here on this earth. I want to live You, and I want to live with You, walk with You,

work with You, and move with You." I pray this every morning, but throughout the day, do I live with the Lord? Do I talk
to people with the Lord; do I work with the Lord; do I move
with the Lord? In a meeting I may speak with the Lord, but
after I return home, I may be another person. I may be
rebuked when I consider whether I am living and moving
with the Lord. This illustrates that we are all far off. Therefore, we should not label people. We should not say that we
are the class of people who live with the Lord, walk with the
Lord, and work with the Lord. There is not such a class. Some
may claim that they are the class of saints who are able to
live in corporate living, but in actuality and practicality they
are not. Why then do we label people? This kind of labeling
offends people, and it indicates that we do not have a spirit
for the weaker ones, for the ones who are inferior to us. It also
indicates that we do not want them. People have often told me
that I am an apostle, but I have never claimed that I am an
apostle. I do not even consider myself qualified to be a pastor.
I am just the same as the other saints. Once we condemn
anyone, we lose the position to take care of that one. Condem-
nation does not stir up our care for others. Who among the
human race is lovable? In the eyes of God, everyone is not
lovable in themselves, yet God still loves them; that is, He
loves the world. I do not prefer to have this kind of fellowship
with you, but I must speak in this way for your sake in order
to shepherd you.

After reading all these portions of the Word, we can see
that we are in a different realm. We say that we are in the
divine and mystical realm, but in actuality we are not. We are
in the natural realm; we are still so natural. Whether or not
we claim that we have a proper corporate living, we may still
be in the flesh, in the old man. We have not been crossed out.
We have not been conformed to Christ's death. To know these
points in the Bible is one thing, but to live them is another. To
say that we live Christ by magnifying Him by the bountiful
supply of the Spirit of Jesus Christ is one thing, but do we
have the reality and practicality of such a life? We all have
to admit that we are on the same level, with only a little
difference in degree. Regardless of how much higher one

seems than another, we are still at the same level. We all need
to see this; then our mouth will be shut. We should not talk
about others; we are the same as they. If we are bothered by
other people's criticizing, our spirit may tell us that we also
criticize others. Then our mouth will be shut. We are the same
as others. One may criticize ten percent, while another criti-
cizes fifteen percent. We are the same; we are all criticizers.

Someone may say that a certain brother should not be an
elder. If not, then who should be an elder? None are qualified.
We must humble ourselves. Pride is the biggest enemy of God.
God resists the proud but gives grace to the humble (James
4:6; 1 Pet. 5:5). Whenever we criticize others, we miss grace
and instead suffer God's resistance. We all must learn to
shepherd one another. This does not mean that since I am
shepherding you, I do not need your shepherding. I need your
shepherding. We all have defects and shortcomings. Everyone
has defects. Therefore, we have to humble ourselves to meet
God's grace. This strengthens our spirit to visit people and
to take care of people regardless of whether they are good
or bad. Regardless of what they are, we must go to visit
them and keep visiting. According to their statistics, the
Jehovah's Witnesses knock on six thousand doors to visit
people in order to gain one. They do this legally, but we do
not. We have no such law forcing others to go out. However, I
am trying my best to help the church to build up the vital
groups with such a shepherding spirit full of love and care for
others.

We need to have this kind of love and go to tell all the
dormant ones who think that the church condemns them that
the church does not condemn anyone. Rather, the church
wants to see all the dormant ones come back. If they all would
come back, I would weep with tears of thanksgiving to the
Lord. The Lord can testify for me that I do not condemn
anyone. We have no qualification to condemn anyone.
Without the Lord's mercy, we would be the same as the
dormant ones. Therefore, we must love them. It all depends
upon love, as the wise king Solomon said, "Love covers all
transgressions" (Prov. 10:12). We love people. We love the
opposers, and we love the top rebels. I really mean it. We love

them and do not hate them. Who am I? I am not qualified to condemn or to hate. Am I perfect? Even the prophet Isaiah, when he saw the Lord, said, "Woe is me, for I am finished / For I am a man of unclean lips, / And in the midst of a people of unclean lips I dwell" (Isa. 6:5). Who is clean today? If we criticize people and say something bad about them, we are not clean.

BEING UNDER THE LORD'S DISCIPLING TO HAVE NO TRUST IN OURSELVES

Recently I have spoken concerning the Lord's discipling. God wants us to be the God-men at the top of the heavenly ladder, but we may not even be on the first rung of the ladder. We are so natural. Therefore, we need to be discipled to see how the Lord lived a divine life by putting His natural life aside. To live a divine life and put off our natural life is divine and mystical.

Often co-workers or elders may come to me and say that they cannot tolerate a certain person. I never instruct them what to do or how to deal with that kind of person. I simply tell them not to do anything. Their situation indicates that they need to be conformed to the death of Christ even more. Sometimes people come to me with tears, but I tell them that their tears are not meaningful. They simply need to go back and be more conformed to the death of Christ and to live the divine life by denying themselves. Today I am more conformed to Christ's death than I have been in sixty years, but my conformation to His death is still not perfected; it is still going on, and I am still under the Lord's discipling. To some extent I am still not a God-man. Often throughout the day I pray to the Lord, "In certain matters, I have not denied myself. My self is still here, and I am too much in myself." I pray this more than once a day. I am under the Lord's discipling. I am a natural man in Adam's race; I am not fully a God-man. I am still a "caterpillar in the cocoon" and not a "butterfly." To be discipled is to be brought from being a "caterpillar" to becoming a "butterfly."

How could Peter, a Jewish fisherman, become a God-man? Peter had never seen a God-man. It is as if the Lord said to him, "Come and follow Me. I will show you a pattern of what a God-man is." Peter watched Him for three and a half years. However, Peter was still like a man of dust with no breath. He did not have the divine life within him until the day of Christ's resurrection. Then he became different because the Spirit was breathed into him. He was enlivened, and he lived a God-man life in practicality and actuality, denying himself and living God. This is the way he was discipled.

We have seen the God-man living, but we have not seen it enough. Peter saw it for three and a half years. Up until the end of the Lord's life in the flesh Peter still had many questions. He may have asked, "What is this man?" Once he told the Lord that he would not deny Him as others would, but the Lord told him that Satan had asked to have him to sift him as wheat and that he would deny Him three times (Luke 22:31-34). In this way Peter was discipled. He spoke as a natural man. He should have said, "Lord, I am no exception. I am the same as all my brothers, and I may be weaker than them. Lord, have mercy upon me and save me." Similarly, we may say that we are able to live in corporate living, but eventually we will find out that we are not. We should have no trust in ourselves.

CHAPTER THREE

BEWARE OF FOUR NEGATIVE FACTORS

A CONCLUDING WORD
REGARDING THE FOREGOING MESSAGES

1. We must have the loving and forgiving heart of our Father God.
2. We must also have the shepherding and seeking spirit of our Savior Christ, with the goal to gain people.
3. We need to remember these two matters and realize them in practicality.

A WORD OF LOVE

I. Beware of:
  A. Ambition:
    1. To be the leader.
    2. To get a place, even a district, for your work.
    3. To captivate people to be your private co-workers.
  B. Pride:
    1. To boast hiddenly of your spiritual capacity.
    2. To exalt yourself and despise others.
    3. To think of yourself more highly than others— Rom. 12:3.
  C. Self-justification and exposing others' failures and defects:
    1. To justify yourself and speak well of your success and merits.
    2. To condemn others, exposing their failures and defects.

D. Not conforming to the death of Christ:
  1. Not absolutely denying your self and bearing the cross.
  2. Not always crucifying your natural man.
  3. Not putting to death your disposition by birth.

Concerning the foregoing messages which I have spoken to the co-workers, elders, and serving ones, we may give the following concluding word: (1) We must have the loving and forgiving heart of our Father God. (2) We must also have the shepherding and seeking spirit of our Savior Christ, with the goal to gain people. (3) We need to remember these two matters and realize them, that is, experience them, in practicality.

BEWARE OF AMBITION

In this message I wish to fellowship with you some further crucial matters. First, we should beware of several factors. These factors are like wolves, roaring lions, and speeding cars on the street that can harm us. The first factor is ambition. What I have written in the accompanying outline is according to my personal experience. I do not mean to say that only you have these negative points and I do not. I also have experienced them. Who does not have ambition? In the Lord's work, the ambition is to be the leader. If you are among the co-workers, you may want to be the leader. If you cannot be the first among them, you may still want to be the "vice-president." Even the sisters who have roommates want to be the leader among them. In the church you may want to be the elder, even the leading elder, the leader of the elders.

Second, your ambition may also be to get a place, even a district, for your work. Who does not have such an ambition? I was with Brother Nee, and I learned of him. I never saw that he was ambitious to get a place, a certain district to be his district or little empire. A district in this sense is a little empire. You may want to be an emperor in your district, with everything under your control and rule and where everyone must listen to you. Who is not like this? I was like this, but the Lord dealt with me. Your ambition may also be to captivate people to be your private co-workers. You may attract, charm, and capture people for this purpose. This means that in your work in the Lord's recovery you have a party in which certain ones who are very close to you have been captivated, attracted, and charmed by you. They appreciate your ability, and they appreciate your capacity, so they stand with you. Then they become your particular co-workers. They are co-workers generally, but in particular they are a certain person's co-workers. Do you not realize that there is such a situation in the Lord's recovery? I have seen this in experience.

Beginning in 1984 I called three urgent conferences of the co-workers and elders. In my opening word I pointed out that among us there is the tendency of division. By this I meant that quite a few capable co-workers in the Lord's recovery liked to keep their district as their empire, and they liked to attract people to be their particular co-workers. We are all co-workers generally, but some became particular co-workers with certain attracting ones. Therefore, I warned you all. After my speaking, one of the co-workers stood to confess that this was the case. However, at that time I realized that his confession was not strong enough. It was very weak, and today he has become a problem in the Lord's recovery. He still claims that he is in the recovery, and he still takes the ground of locality. He protests that his meeting is a local church, and he declares that he is one with Brother Lee. He accepts my ministry, and he receives standing orders of the books of the Living Stream Ministry even until today. Recently, he spoke to me for close to one hour to explain his stand. I told him I felt that it was not the Lord's timing to respond to him at that time. Later, after further consideration with the Lord, I felt that I had received a clear word and that it was the Lord's timing to respond. I felt to tell him, "You are a division, and whatever you do in your place is a division because you cut your meeting off from all the churches in the recovery. Moreover, you like to visit the rebellious ones and stand with them. You should realize that all the churches are one Body. You cannot stand alone, separate from the other churches. If you do, you are a division." In Corinth some said, "I am of Paul, and I of Apollos, and I of Cephas, and I of Christ" (1 Cor. 1:12). Paul condemned them for this. Even if you say that you are of Christ, that is a division. It is as if Paul said to them, "Is Christ divided? Why do you say that you are of Paul? Do not be of me. I am of you, and we all are of Christ." First Corinthians 1 shows us that there should not be any differences among us. No one is of Cephas, no one is of Apollos, no one is of Paul, the highest apostle, and no one is even of Christ separately from others. We all are of Christ, who is not divided.

Our fallen disposition by birth always likes to captivate people. If someone can do a work for the Lord, he may like to attract people. He may like to charm them and captivate them, and if he succeeds in captivating others, the captivated ones become members of his little party. In the Lord's recovery there is the possibility of having such a party. If you have the opportunity and the time, you may do this. You have not done this because you have not had the opportunity, the condition, and the situation, but when you do have the opportunity, you may do it. This is the first "underground gopher" that damages the Lord's recovery. You may have been damaged by this. Within you there may be this very strong hidden "gopher." I consider this as the first problem.

BEWARE OF PRIDE

We should also beware of pride. To be proud is to boast. You may not boast openly, but you may boast hiddenly of your spiritual capacity, ability, and capability. Sometimes people boast in this way, saying, "See what capacity I have. Can your capacity or ability compare with mine?" Even someone without much capacity may still boast that he can do what others cannot. To be proud is also to exalt yourself and despise others. Again I ask, "Who does not exalt themselves and despise others?" I have learned this lesson, I have experienced all these things, and I have seen the situations. Therefore, I do have a burden within me to speak to you all, and I feel that this is the time to speak a word of love concerning ambition, pride, self-justification, and not being conformed to the death of Christ.

To be proud is also to think of yourself more highly than others. To be sure, this is a common illness among all Christians. Therefore, Paul charged us, saying, "For I say, through the grace given to me, to every one who is among you, not to think more highly of himself than he ought to think, but to think so as to be sober-minded, as God has apportioned to each a measure of faith" (Rom. 12:3). Although the Lord has been gone for nearly two thousand years, why does it seem that almost nothing has been accomplished for the building up of the Body? It is simply because of all these "gophers." Paul was very aware of the matter of pride. He said that a new convert should not be appointed to bear responsibility because, being blinded with pride, he may fall into the judgment suffered by the devil (1 Tim. 3:6). I have seen this. In appointing certain ones into responsibility there is the risk of spoiling them with pride.

BEWARE OF SELF-JUSTIFICATION
AND EXPOSING OTHERS' FAILURES AND DEFECTS

We must also beware of self-justification and exposing others' failures and defects. We often like to justify ourselves and expose others' shortages, mistakes, and defects. Among us some are very particular in doing this, justifying themselves all the time. We never hear that certain ones condemn themselves, but rather they are always justifying themselves while exposing others' failures and defects. To be snared in this way is to justify yourself and speak well of your success and merits. It is to speak of how you succeeded in this work or in that work and to speak well of all your good points. I wish to put this message into your mind so that you may keep it in your memory. Then you can look and see our situation. The situation in the Lord's recovery is exactly like this.

As I have said before, the spirit of not shepherding and seeking others and being without love and forgiveness is spreading in the recovery everywhere. I believe that not having the Father's loving and forgiving heart and not having the Savior's shepherding and seeking spirit is the reason for our barrenness. I realize that you all work hard, but there is almost no fruit. The Lord says, "By the fruit the tree is known" (Matt. 12:33), but we are a tree without any fruit. Everywhere among us barrenness is very prevailing. A good, gentle, pastor may not have a particular gift, such as the gift of speaking; he may simply visit people and welcome them when they come to his meeting, but according to statistics, he will have a ten-percent yearly increase. We, however, do not *[handwritten margin notes: Bearing fruit is not about method, but our heart → for our self? (proud, ambition, self-justification & experiencing the cross) Only He is the capable one.]*

[handwritten margin notes: To live Christ. A fruitful life. → for the Lord (Shepherding & seeking spirit)]

have even a ten-percent increase. Can you see how barren we are? Many of you are good speakers, knowing the higher truths. The truths we hold are much higher than those in Christianity. However, we do not have fruit because we are lacking in the Father's loving and forgiving heart and the Son's shepherding and seeking spirit. We condemn and regulate others rather than shepherd and seek them. We are short of love and shepherding. These are the vital factors for us to bear fruit, that is, to gain people. I am very concerned for our full-time training. Do we train the young ones to gain people or to regulate people? We have to reconsider our ways, as Haggai said (1:5). Our way is not right; something is wrong.

We often condemn others, exposing their failures and defects. We must admit that to speak well of ourselves and to expose others' defects is our natural disposition. Our disposition is like this by birth. There is no need for us to speak about others' defects, but we may simply like to do it. Many times the brothers come together and speak about others' weak points, defects, and failures. I have learned the lesson to be fearful and trembling about speaking of others' defects. In the world the legal term for this is *defamation*. Why do we need to speak in a defaming way? However, nearly all of us do this. Because by the Lord's mercy and grace I have learned the lesson, it is very hard for you to hear me speak of anyone's defects. Whenever I speak of others' shortages, I am condemned, saying to myself, "Do you not have shortages?" The Pharisees and scribes brought a sinful woman to the Lord and said, "In the law, Moses commanded us to stone such women. What then do you say?" (John 8:5). First, the Lord stooped down. This was to show them humility. He did not stand, saying, "What! Do you come to Me? Let Me tell you something!" The Lord stooped down to write on the ground. According to my study of the Bible, I believe that what the Lord wrote was, "Who is without sin?" It is as if He said, "There is no doubt that she is sinful, and she got caught. But are you without sin?" They charged the Lord to say something, so He said, "He who is without sin among you, let him be the first to throw a stone at her" (v. 7). Their conscience was caught. Everyone, beginning from the older ones, the experienced ones, was smitten. Who is without sin? When you speak of others' shortages, do you not have shortages? Yet according to our disposition by birth, to speak about others' defects is our "hobby." Do you like to expose your own shortages? You do not; you like to cover them.

BEWARE OF NOT CONFORMING
TO THE DEATH OF CHRIST

We must also beware of not conforming to the death of Christ. We should always conform ourselves to His death, but often we do not. We should be warned. Beware of this! Matthew 16:24 says, "If anyone wants to come after Me, let him deny himself and take up his cross and follow Me." To not conform to the death of Christ is to not absolutely deny your self, not others' self, and bear the cross. To bear the cross is to keep your self on the cross. Do not leave the cross. That is the right place for your self to be. Not to conform to the death of Christ is also not to always crucify your natural man. Often when people contact me, their every word is out of the natural man. Sometimes we crucify our natural man, but most of the time we do not. Not to conform to the death of Christ is also not to put to death your disposition by birth. A person may boast of his race or that he is from a certain country with a prideful spirit and an air of superiority. Some even boast of their disposition by birth. Sometimes I have wanted to say, "Don't you know that I am a quick person?" However, as soon as this word comes to the tip of my tongue, I must swallow it. Honestly speaking, who is not like this?

This is the word of love which I am burdened to pass on to you all. Ambition, pride, self-justification, and not conforming to the death of Christ are four "gophers." If we deal with these four matters, the Lord's recovery will immediately have a revival, and within one month we will see fruit as the result. Trouble after trouble has come to the Lord's recovery over the years simply because of these four matters. Some co-workers were ambitious, intending to gain a place or a person, using my name to give people the impression that Brother Lee sent them. Did I send them or not? Yes, in a positive sense I did say, "That place needs your help." Whether or not that was my sending, I do not know, but even if that was a sending, I did not send you to control others, to subdue others, with my name. I have suffered very much because of this. Some people have thought, "Brother Lee is such a person. He would not come to control us, but he would control us through certain other persons." This has happened in the recovery. Because of this, some people not only rejected this one who utilized my name, but some also rejected me even the more. They said, "Why is Brother Lee so bad?" Actually, the one who went there to utilize my name and misrepresent me caused the trouble. Such a thing transpired two or three years ago among us, and the trouble still remains.

Dear saints, I know that you all love the Lord, and I know that you love the recovery. I also believe that you receive my ministry from the Lord, but there is a big "but." If you would not deal with these four gophers, everything else means nothing. We may have some capacity, but our capacity will be annulled, annihilated, by our disposition, our pride, and our unwillingness to put our disposition by birth on the cross. The Lord has blessed His recovery and is still blessing it. Look at the spread of the recovery. However, our situation is like that of Song of Songs 2:15, which says, "Catch the foxes for us, / The little foxes, / That ruin the vineyards / While our vineyards are in blossom." This is my concern, and this is why I purposed to speak these few messages. Our carelessness in these four matters and our failure to beware of these four things is an opportunity afforded to Satan to spoil the blossoming of the Lord's recovery today. The enemy is subtle. We should not be ignorant of his devices.

OUR NEED FOR THE CROSS
ALONG WITH THE HIGH PEAKS OF THE TRUTH

The Lord is giving us the high peaks of the truth, and we appreciate them and are learning to speak the same thing, but on the hidden side, these four negative factors are still remaining among us. This will annul whatever benefit we receive from the high peaks of the divine truths. This is my concern. Doctors are always concerned about hidden germs.

My burden is to kill these germs. I have the deep realization that the Lord has had mercy on His recovery to unveil to us all the deep points in His Word. Recently, I spoke a word to explain the four *ins* in John 14. According to verse 17, the Spirit of reality is not only with us but also in us. Verse 20 continues by saying, "I am in My Father, and you in Me, and I in you." The *in* of verse 17 is the totality of the three *ins* in verse 20. God is three: The Father is the source, the Son is the course, and the Spirit is the flow. This can be compared to a river of water, which has a fountain, a spring, and a flow. It is not that there are three kinds of water; it is that the flow is the consummation of the water. The Spirit as the flowing river is the consummation of the Triune God as living water. This can be strongly proved by 2 Corinthians 13:14, which says, "The grace of the Lord Jesus Christ and the love of God and the fellowship of the Holy Spirit be with you all." In actuality, there are not three elements in this blessing. There is only the element of grace and the element of love. What, then, is the third item? It is the transportation, the fellowship, of the elements of grace and love. All cargo needs to be transported. The fellowship of the Spirit is the consummation of the grace of Christ and the love of God. This is an illustration of the high peaks of the truth that we have. I have a burden from the Lord to write a further crystallization-study of Romans. I will give a number of messages on reigning in life by the abundance of the grace that we have received. However, I am concerned that if these four "gophers" are not dealt with among us, the more the deeper truths and higher peaks of the divine revelation are released among us, the more proud we will become. All across this country all the churches are speaking the same thing, which are the high peaks. But the gophers are here, so I feel I must do something.

I will repeat and stress these matters more strongly in the upcoming international conference of co-workers and elders on the full ministry of Christ in His three stages: the stage of His incarnation, the stage of His inclusion, and the stage of His intensification. Intensification is not only to give you more of the Spirit; it is also to cause you to be conformed sevenfold to the death of Christ. Your being crucified, your denial of the self, and your bearing of the cross should be intensified sevenfold. You cannot preach only the side of the Spirit without the side of the cross. If there is no cross, there is no Spirit. *Hymns,* #279, written by Brother Nee, tells us that we first need the cross and then the Spirit. Verse 5 says, "When we see the ripened harvest / Of the golden country-side, / We may know that many seeds have / Fallen to the earth and died." The blossoming harvest is due to seeds falling into the earth to die. The shell of our natural humanity must be broken. First is Golgotha, the cross, and second is Pentecost, the Spirit (stanza 1). Without crossing through the Jordan River, that is, the cross, how can you enter into the good land (stanza 4)? On the one hand, I feel burdened to minister the high peaks of the truth concerning the full ministry of Christ in the flesh, as the life-giving Spirit, and as the sevenfold intensified life-giving Spirit. On the other hand, the Lord has charged me to minister the cross.

Your natural man, your self, can be fed with the high-peak truths. They can make you more ambitious because they give you more capacity, and they can make you prouder because you now have the high peaks. Many people have never heard these things, but today you are hearing them. When you go out to preach and speak them, everyone will welcome you. This will feed you, not in a positive sense but in a negative sense. This feeding is negative. Good doctors who feed their patients first take care to kill the germs. If they do not kill the germs, their feeding will be full of germs. The northern Chinese often eat dumplings with garlic and vinegar. Both garlic and vinegar kill germs. Moreover, vinegar is also good for digestion. The germs are killed, and the people have good digestion. The dumpling-eaters do not become sick because they are protected by the germ-killers. The garlic and vinegar make their dumplings not only tasteful but safe. I cannot feed you the high-peak truths without "garlic." I must minister some garlic and vinegar to you even though this is not sweet. People may prefer honey, but honey is prohibited in the Bible. In the Old Testament the people were not allowed to put honey in the meal offering; rather, they put in salt, which kills germs (Lev.

2:11, 13). I am afraid that in speaking so many high-peak truths, I have fed you with honey. This will eventually kill you. I must put in some salt; we all have to be salted.

I am concerned for the Lord's recovery. Nothing else on this earth is upon my heart, especially at the end of my course. I must treasure the end of my course. I want to do the best to minister the all-inclusive Christ and the compound, all-inclusive, consummated Spirit, but not without the cross. I will minister "dumplings" to you, but I must put strong garlic in them with much vinegar, the more the better, and the more the safer. I am not so capable to expose all the problems, but I am under the Lord's dealing. The Lord has given me a thorn. I thank Him for this. I have told Him, "Lord, I love Your dealing. I love this thorn."

BEING CONCERNED FOR THE LORD'S RECOVERY
AND NOT FOR OUR OWN WORK

Our full-time training should not have a purpose to keep the trainees in Anaheim to do a work in Anaheim or in Southern California. We should send them back to the places from which they came. Recently I heard certain ones complaining that they spend much labor to gain people, and they send them to the training for four terms at a great cost, but eventually the trainees do not come back. They are retained in Anaheim. We should not convince the trainees to stay in Anaheim after their four terms. This is to be ambitious, to get people for our work and not for the work of the Lord's recovery. I am not for this. I am for the Lord's recovery. The training I set up has the intention to train people from all the nations. I have strongly said that all the foreigners should go back to their country after being trained. A number of trainees from New Zealand wanted to stay, but I encouraged them to go back to New Zealand. Some like to keep more people on the campuses in Southern California, but what about the campuses in other countries? Something wrong is hidden here, and some have complained about it. Do not think that I have the intention to keep the trainees here. If I have such a concept, I should be condemned. This would

Mon 3-5 p.m. Lord's move in Europe, helps all the ~~saints~~ saints to not just focusing on our own district, our own locality.

BEWARE OF FOUR NEGATIVE FACTORS   47

mean that I am ambitious to get all the best ones to come to Anaheim.

Be careful; do not keep people for your campus. The enemy does things subtly, so the Lord says, "Watch and pray that you may not enter into temptation" (Matt. 26:41). We are short of watching and praying, so the subtle one has come in to deceive us. Some like to keep the good ones in their own city, and they complain that the training assigns too many good ones to the other cities. You may say, "We are keeping the trainees so that we can gain more people." However, to the Lord every place is the same. Whether He gains people in one place or in another is the same. Why do you want to keep people in your place? It is simply for yourself. This is ambition; it is something hidden. Do not think that I do not love the church in your place. My heart is for the recovery, and by "the recovery" I mean the Lord's move on the whole earth. I am for the churches, not merely for one church. Therefore, when I see these things, my heart aches.

You must learn to condemn and reject your self to the uttermost and simply take care of the Lord's interest, of His recovery, and not your work. Then the Lord will honor you. You do not need to go out to advertise. To the Lord money does not mean anything. If we afford Him a way, He will provide. After the Gulf War in 1991, we were ready to afford the Lord a way for His move in Russia, so right away He put His blessing upon us. Where did the saints come from who went to Russia? Many simply wanted to go. This was the Lord's doing; it was not my doing. I did not go out to convince anyone to give, to go, or to pray, but many prayers were poured out for this move. Now we can see the result. Thousands of the leading cities in Russia, some with over one million people, have been reached by our publications. I have read some of the responses of the Russian people. They ask for more books by Brother Nee and myself. They realize that we are one, and they do not want others' writings. As of this time we have sent seventy Americans and sixty Chinese, and about seventy Russians have been raised up locally and trained to serve with their full time. This is the result of the

[margin note: Not our own preference.]

Lord's move, not the result of my work. I am not able to do this much. The Lord has done it.

I have received many letters to which I did not reply, because I knew your concern was merely for your district. This is for your work, and I am not for that. The Lord is spreading widely throughout the world and around the globe. Therefore, I would like to see that all of you are for the concern of the Lord's recovery, not for the work in your district.

CHAPTER FOUR (Assignment to read)

BE RIGHT IN FOLLOWING OTHERS

II. Be right in following others:
  A. Be careful in following any co-workers whom you appreciate and to whom you are attracted:
    1. He should be a person loving the Lord, living for the Lord, and renouncing his self, natural life, preference, and ambition.
    2. He must hold the complete revelation of the entire holy Scriptures properly without any twisting and deforming.
    3. He must be one who endeavors to keep the oneness of the Spirit, the oneness of the universal Body, by taking the unique ground of the local church.
  B. Be strongly discerning in the accepting of the divine revelation according to the holy Scriptures:
    1. The accepting of the divine revelation must be governed by:
      a. The eternal economy of God as the basic principle.
      b. Christ as the centrality and universality of God's eternal economy.
      c. The Body of Christ which consummates the New Jerusalem as the divine goal of the processed and consummated Triune God.
    2. The application of the divine truths must avoid:
      a. Uplifting any basic truths, such as the three sections of sanctification, the designation of Christ as the seed of David to be the first-born Son of God, the acknowledgment of the

fact that "I am of Christ," etc., to cause divisions that divide Christ, including His Body (1 Cor. 1:11-13a).

b. Neglecting any subordinate truths or stressing any of them, which leads toward the direction of division that divides the Body of Christ.

Prayer: Lord, we thank You for Your mercy and for Your grace. Lord, without Your mercy, we could not have gone on up to this day. Lord, we need Your forgiveness, Your washing away of all our dirt and defects with Your blood. Lord, we can stand here before You not on our perfection but on the blood that overcomes the accuser. We trust in Your mercy, and we trust in Your blood. Lord, this morning give us another chance for fellowship that we would be open to one another. We are open to You. Lord, come and fellowship with us, and grant us Your fellowship that we may have the freedom to fellowship with one another. Lord, give us understanding and save us from any kind of misunderstanding. Lord, give us a clear word, a clear understanding, and a clear receiving. May nothing be stumbling. Lord, save us from making mistakes. It is so easy for us to make mistakes. Lord, in our being there is the capacity to always make mistakes. We trust in You to deliver us that we may learn how to reject, how to deny, ourselves. Amen.

I hope that you would keep the outline of this message in front of you, hanging it on your wall or standing it on your desk. You should read it once a day for a month.

In the previous message we covered the first part of my word of love. In that part we covered four matters: ambition, pride, self-justification and exposing others' failures and defects, and not conforming to the death of Christ. To conform to the death of Christ relates to the self, the natural man, and the disposition. We must deny our self, condemn our natural life, and forget about our disposition by birth. Self, the natural life or the natural man, and disposition by birth are like three evil brothers. We all have our own disposition by birth. One person may have been born a quick person. His quickness is his disposition, and his quick disposition is by his birth. He did not learn it; he was simply born that way. Another person may be a slow person. He also did not learn his slowness from others; his slow disposition is by birth. This is the fourth "gopher." These four "gophers"—ambition, pride, self-justification, and the self, that is, the natural man in our disposition by birth—are destroying us every day. I have realized this through many years of experiences. I have been with the saints, serving the Lord since He raised me up to speak for Him in 1932. At that time, a little church was raised up through me. I could not reject my responsibility to take care of that church. So from that year, sixty-four years ago, I began to be with the serving ones. In these sixty-four years I have seen many things, I have gone through many things, I have experienced many things, and I have suffered quite much. I have suffered from others' ambition, pride, self-justification, self, natural man, and disposition by birth.

Our history spans not only sixty-four years but nearly two thousand years. I have experienced some things myself, and I have come to know the same things through my study of church history and the biographies and autobiographies of spiritual giants. Nearly all the biographies are helpful. I read George Müller's autobiography. Actually, that is his daily diary, the daily record of his living. It is a very helpful book, and I received much help from it. I also read the biography of Hudson Taylor, which was written by his daughter-in-law. That also was very helpful. However, all the biographies and autobiographies are small windows through which I can see these four gophers—ambition, pride, self-justification, and the biggest one, our natural man, our self involved with our natural disposition. The outcome of all these four gophers is division. These, not other things, are the real sources of all the denominations. Hudson Taylor was a young missionary sent to China. He was working in Ningpo in the Chekiang province along the coast. After returning to England, as he was sitting by the seashore looking toward the east, he could not forget China. While he was sitting and praying, the Lord burdened him to go back to China, but not to the coast. Nearly all the missions in China were only along the coast. The Lord burdened him to go inland, to the interior. That was wonderful, but Hudson Taylor still had his defects. He declared and proclaimed that the churches established by his missionaries were not denominational; therefore, they did not have a name. That was true, but they still called themselves the churches of the China Inland Mission.

We all have defects. Martin Luther was great, but his defect was also great. At first he was a hero, but eventually he was not a hero. He was afraid of persecution by the Catholic Church, so he relied upon the king of Germany. That defect initiated the beginning of the so-called national churches, the churches of a nation, especially in Northern Europe. There are the Church of Germany, the Church of Denmark, the Church of Sweden, the Church of Norway, the Church of England, and the Church of Holland. All those national churches take their king or queen as the head of the church. The head of the Church of England today is the queen. Strictly speaking, whether you are Chinese, American, or German, to be an Episcopalian is to be a British subject. Today in Germany every citizen has to pay a church tax to the government. Luther, a great hero, made a great mistake.

I saw all these things. Among us, Brother Nee took the lead to read all these books. He exhaustively collected all the church histories, autobiographies, and biographies of the spiritual giants. In this way, he collected all the views and could make a conclusion. I received much help from Brother Nee. I also have personally been in many situations, contacting the saints, both the saints in the denominations and the saints in the Lord's recovery. I have seen a good number of Chinese preachers who gained a name, who became famous, and many of them came into the Lord's recovery. On the one hand, they knew that the recovery had the truth, and they were right according to the truths that the recovery holds. On the other hand, these four "gophers" destroyed them, and not one has remained. Some remained for a period of time, but eventually they all left. The history among us proves that those who became somewhat capable, possessing a certain "spiritual capacity," eventually became a problem.

Soon after I first came to this country, we held the first summer training on the matter of the kingdom. A certain brother who was a traveling Southern Baptist preacher came to every meeting to listen to the messages. He was convinced and, in a sense, was captivated. He left the Southern Baptist Church and came among us. It was he who first brought me to Texas in 1963. The doors in Texas were opened through

him. The first meetings we held there were in the small town
of Tyler. There were about five hundred people who came to
listen to me, including some leading ones, and they accepted
my teaching. They said, "This is right. We must be this kind
of local church." I stayed there for a short time, and while
I was in New York, they called me and asked me to return.
They said, "We have many here who are ready to meet as
the local church, and we do not know how to do it. Please
come to help us." I went back to them, and I stayed in the
home of a rich man, whose wife was very eloquent and active
in loving the Lord, but eventually I realized that they were
not the ones who could take this way. The first group of people
the Lord Jesus called did not have doctoral degrees; they
were not like Nicodemus. According to the record of the
New Testament, Nicodemus is mentioned only three times.
He was probably not among the one hundred twenty. The first
three of the twelve apostles—Peter, John, and James—were
Galilean fishermen. Eventually, the one who brought me to
Texas only stayed with us for six years, from 1963 to 1969.
In 1969 he wanted to start his own way, using my teachings, especially from *The Tree of Life*. Even though he started
his own way, he still came occasionally to Elden Hall to
pick up our outlines and to see what I was putting out. I
gave him a small warning, but that was all. He is still active
today. I have seen many such things. Now you have been
brought into the Lord's recovery. We thank the Lord for
this, but if you do not cooperate with the Lord to deal with
ambition, pride, and self-justification, and if you are not
conformed to the death of Christ, the outcome among us will
be division.

In 1964 in Los Angeles we met several different groups of
people. One was a Pentecostal group, and one was an inner-
life group that followed the teaching of T. Austin-Sparks.
After they heard my messages, the leaders of these groups
implored me, saying, "Brother Lee, now we realize the way we
should take. Let us come together to practice the Body life
according to Romans 12." I said that this was wonderful, but
if they were to practice Romans 12, they should not forget
Romans 14. That was the first time this word on this subject

issued forth from my mouth. I told them that if anyone wants to practice Romans 12 concerning the Body of Christ, they have to be reminded of Romans 14. In Romans 14 Paul was very liberal. According to Paul, we must receive all believers, whether they keep the Sabbath, the seventh day, or the Lord's Day, and regardless of what kind of food they eat, whether they are vegetarian or eat meat. We must receive them because God has received them. This is to be very general. They said, "We will do it. We will be general." Therefore, we started to meet together. Afterward, I had to go to New York to attend an interview with the immigration office for my permanent residence, and when I returned, some of them came to me. One said, "Brother Lee, a certain young sister in our meeting plays the tambourine. I cannot take that." This brother said that he approved of playing the piano. I asked him, "In the eyes of God what is the difference between a piano and a tambourine?" He admitted that there is no difference. I said, "If you can accept the piano, why can't you accept the tambourine?" One by one others came to me in the same way.

Generally speaking, there have been only two or three occasions of rebellion among us, but in actuality, there have been many. One brother who was very close to me often traveled with me, and he opened his home to me as if it were my own. However, when I began to have the life-study trainings in which I released thirty messages, he became dissenting. He could not agree with this way. He started to have the Lord's table with young children, serving them the table in his home, and he claimed that his way was the right way to practice the church life. Eventually, he also gave up the recovery. I have seen many things like this. Now you can see why I want to give you this word of love. You must beware of four things: ambition, pride, self-justification, and the self, the natural man, the disposition. Every human being is a self-justifying person. We only know to justify ourselves; it is very hard to recognize others' perfection. We were all born this way, but we must not let this "gopher" remain within us. We must reject our self-justification. This is the first group of problems in the church life.

BEING CAREFUL IN FOLLOWING
ANY CO-WORKER WHOM WE APPRECIATE
AND TO WHOM WE ARE ATTRACTED

Second, we must be right in following others. First Corinthians 1 was written to deal with the divisions in the church at Corinth. Verses 10-12 say, "Now I beseech you, brothers, through the name of our Lord Jesus Christ, that you all speak the same thing and that there be no divisions among you, but that you be attuned in the same mind and in the same opinion. For it has been made clear to me concerning you, my brothers, by those of the household of Chloe, that there are strifes among you. Now I mean this, that each of you says, I am of Paul, and I of Apollos, and I of Cephas, and I of Christ." Verse 10 says that we should speak the same thing. How can we all speak the same thing? In 1 Timothy 1:3-4 Paul exhorts Timothy to remain in Ephesus to charge certain ones not to teach different things but to speak the same thing, which is God's economy. God's economy is the only thing we can speak in the same way, and we must speak it in the same way. The entire book of 1 Corinthians reveals God's economy. The second half of chapter one says that Christ is God's power and God's wisdom (vv. 18-25), and this Christ has been given to us to be our righteousness for the past, sanctification for the present, and redemption for the future (vv. 26-31). Christ is all to us; this is God's economy, the one thing which we speak.

Some in Corinth said they were of Paul (v. 12). This is to follow Paul out of preference for him. Paul in his wisdom first condemned himself. It is as if he said, "Do you say that you are of me, Paul? No, I reject and condemn this." Eventually, at the end of chapter three he said that he was of them (v. 22). Today someone may say, "Brother Lee, I am of you." It seems that I should be happy because I have gained a follower to stand with me. However, this is wrong. Some liked to follow Apollos, and some liked to follow Cephas. Others were very proud and said, "You are of Paul, Apollos, or Cephas, but that is wrong. I do not belong to Paul, Apollos, or Cephas. I belong to Christ; I am of Christ." To say, "I am of Christ" in the way of division was to make themselves different, even superior.

Paul condemned even this kind of saying. He asked, "Is Christ divided?" (1:13). This shows us that we must be right in following others. We cannot avoid having so many of us together, especially today as the modern conveniences make the globe small. Without gathering together, where is the Body life and where is the practice of the church? We have to come together. But we have many different persons with many backgrounds and cultures, so we have to be careful. If you follow the wrong person, you will damage yourself, and you will damage that person. Your following of a person wrongly is a destruction to the one whom you follow.

You must be careful in following any co-worker whom you appreciate and to whom you are attracted. If you do not appreciate a person, you will not follow him. First you appreciate someone, and then you are attracted to him. I have seen this among us here in America. I have spoken a word of love directly to these kinds of brothers. I have warned them to not do this kind of work. Wherever you go, you may become the superior one. You may be good; there is nothing wrong with that. You do have a capacity which might be higher than others'. However, you should avoid doing a work to attract people to follow you. We all have to see this. Such a one who makes himself attractive is wrong already, and if you are attracted to follow him, you help him to be wrong. You destroy yourself, and you also destroy him. I have seen this. I warned one person more than five times. I said, "Brother, you should not do this." I warned him in a very private way, but now my speaking is public. I have spoken publicly to you because there is such a danger that you may appreciate certain persons. I do not like to hear that you appreciate me, that you feel I am right and you follow me. If you appreciate the truths I have put out, I thank the Lord, but if you appreciate me, that is wrong. Be careful in following any co-worker whom you appreciate and to whom you are attracted. To be one with another co-worker in this way is wrong. Regardless of what the reason is for this oneness, you are wrong. We all are one. We do not have parties. Do not say, I am one with Brother So-and-so. To be one with anyone in particular is wrong. To be one with all the saints is right.

First Corinthians 1:10 speaks of being attuned in the same mind and in the same opinion. Concerning the word *attuned,* footnote 4 in the Recovery Version says:

> The same word in Greek that is translated *mending* in Matthew 4:21. It means *to repair, to restore, to adjust, to mend, making a broken thing thoroughly complete, joined perfectly together.* The Corinthian believers as a whole were divided, broken. They needed to be mended in order to be joined perfectly together that they might be in harmony, having the same mind and the same opinion to speak the same thing, that is, Christ and His cross.

To be attuned is to be joined together, as a piano is tuned to give a proper harmony and melody. Learn to be attuned, learn to be adjusted, and learn to be corrected. The harmony in the Lord's recovery can be maintained only by dealing with the four "gophers"—ambition, pride, self-justification, and you yourself as the self, the natural man, your disposition by birth.

Being a Person
Loving the Lord, Living for the Lord,
and Renouncing His Self, Natural Life,
Preference, and Ambition

One whom we follow should be a person loving the Lord, living for the Lord, and renouncing his self, natural life, preference, and ambition. Regardless of how good one is and how high his spiritual capacity might be, you must ask, "Is this one to whom I have been attracted a person who all the time renounces his self, his natural life, his preference, and ambition?" Ambition is sometimes hidden, but every man's preference is always exposed. If one says he likes to do things in a certain way, that is his preference. Sometimes people have exposed their preference by coming to me and saying, "Brother Lee, you are too loose. We know what the right way is, but when the brothers fellowship with you and propose a certain way, you always agree with them." This is true; I have often done this. Deep within I know what the right way is, but there is not only one way to do something. I have illustrated this by the way we drive a car. Once three brothers intended to drive to Los Angeles. The first one proposed a way to go, the second one proposed a better way, and the third one proposed yet another way that would save time. The three argued for so long that by the time they finished arguing, they could have been there no matter what way they went. This is why I often say to others, "Simply do it any way." It is the same in the way we take care of our training. People consider that this is Brother Lee's training, but in actuality I let others do many small things in any way they can; any way is right. In order to keep a peaceful spirit, we all have to learn how to give in. In order to keep peace, do not argue and have no preference. Do not think that it saves time to discuss everything first. Many husbands have learned this. Many times to discuss things with their wives takes twice as long as doing the thing. To discuss not only wastes time, but it often causes the husband and wife to become angry with each other. The best way is for a husband to say, "Dear, whatever you say is good; go ahead and do it." It is not easy to be this way.

If you are a strong man, no one can change your preference. You insist that you are right and that your way is the right way. This is wrong. In the church life in the Lord's recovery we all have to learn how to give in, even if it means that we suffer. You may ask, "Don't we need to protect the recovery?" Dear ones, if you try to protect the recovery, that is your mistake. Can you protect the recovery? Brother Nee said once that no one can protect God's glory. Only God Himself can protect His glory. Who are we? To insist upon your preference is a real damage to the recovery. Your intention may be to protect the recovery from mistakes, but in actuality your insistence on your preference is the biggest mistake. To give in is right. We can only do this by the Lord's grace. Without the Lord's grace, who can give up his preference? No one can. Those dear ones especially who are born with a strong character must be aware of their strong character in insisting on their preference.

Being a Person Holding the Complete Revelation of the Entire Holy Scriptures Properly without Any Twisting and Deforming

One whom we follow must hold the complete revelation of the entire holy Scriptures properly without any twisting and deforming. The word *twist* is used in 2 Peter 3:15-16, in which Peter says, "Our beloved brother Paul, according to the wisdom given to him, wrote to you, as also in all his letters, speaking in them concerning these things, in which some things are hard to understand, which the unlearned and unstable twist, as also the rest of the Scriptures, to their own destruction." According to my observation, deforming is different from twisting. To deform the truth is simply to change it a little or add something. To put a small cap on my head, for example, deforms the appearance of my head. Do not cut off anything from the truth, and do not add anything to it. Take the truth as it is. If you do not take the truth as it is, you may say that you are not twisting the Scriptures. Yes, you may not twist them, but you are deforming them. Concerning one whom you follow, you must check how he handles the truth.

Being One Who Endeavors to Keep the Oneness of the Spirit, the Oneness of the Universal Body, by Taking the Unique Ground of the Local Church

One whom you follow must be one who endeavors to keep the oneness of the Spirit, the oneness of the universal Body, by taking the unique ground of the local church. Everyone agrees with the speaking about the oneness of the universal Body. Who can deny this truth? In Christ we all are one Body universally. *Universally* refers not only to space but also time. Paul lived nearly two thousand years ago, but we are one with him. Moreover, a brother in Germany lives thousands of miles away, but we are still one with him. This is universal oneness, in which we are one with all believers. However, even if you say that you are for the oneness of the

Body, to not take the unique ground of the local church is strong evidence that you do not care for the oneness of the Body. In actuality, you are one with no one; you are one only with yourself. You yourself should first be clear about the oneness; otherwise, you will be deceived.

BEING STRONGLY DISCERNING
IN THE ACCEPTING OF THE DIVINE REVELATION
ACCORDING TO THE HOLY SCRIPTURES

The Accepting of the Divine Revelation Being Governed by the Eternal Economy of God, by Christ, and by the Body of Christ for the New Jerusalem

We must be strongly discerning in the accepting of the divine revelation according to the holy Scriptures. The accepting of the divine revelation must be governed by three things. The first is the eternal economy of God as the basic principle. Many Christians today argue with one another, but very few know that in the Bible there is such a thing as the eternal economy of God. The accepting of the divine revelation must also be governed by Christ as the centrality and universality of God's eternal economy. God has an economy, and Christ is the centrality and universality of this economy. In other words, Christ is everything in God's economy.

I have spoken strongly concerning God's economy in the last ten or more years, and I have published three or four books on God's economy. The first, *The Economy of God,* was published in 1968. It did not speak of God's economy as a plan but of God's economy in our being concerning our spirit, our mind, our will, and our emotion. I spoke further on God's economy beginning from Stuttgart, Germany in 1984 and continuing on the east coast of the United States and in Irving, Texas. This speaking was published as *God's New Testament Economy.* Today if you would ask me to speak something basic, I cannot stay away from God's economy. Anything that is basic must be according to God's economy. The hub and the rim of the eternal economy of God is Christ. God has no plan outside of Christ. Christ is everything. The term *Christ as the centrality and universality* was used by Brother Nee since

1934 when he gave messages concerning Christ being all in all. I received much help from those messages.

The accepting of the divine revelation must also be governed by the Body of Christ which consummates the New Jerusalem as the divine goal of the processed and consummated Triune God. John 4:14 says, "The water that I will give him will become in him a spring of water gushing up into eternal life." The Triune God is a fountain emerging to be a spring and gushing up to be a river flowing into eternal life. The fountain is God the Father, the spring is God the Son, and the river is God the Spirit flowing as living water into eternal life. For more than fifty years I tried to understand the phrase *into eternal life*, but I was unable. In recent days, however, I have come to know the meaning. *Into eternal life* does not mean to enter into eternal life. It means to become the eternal life. The flowing of the Father as the fountain, the Son as the spring, and the Spirit as the river eventually becomes the eternal life, which is the New Jerusalem. The entire Bible shows us that our God is the flowing God. God flowed in the Father as the fountain, and the Father emerged, was manifested, to be the Son as the spring, and the gushing river is the Spirit. The issue, the consummation, of this flowing is the New Jerusalem. From Genesis to Revelation the entire Bible speaks only about this flowing Triune God, and the issue of Their flowing is the New Jerusalem. Just as a man is the consummation of the human life, the consummation of the divine life is the New Jerusalem.

The Application of the Divine Truths
Avoiding Uplifting Any Basic Truths and
Neglecting Any Subordinate Truths
or Stressing Any of Them

The application of the divine truths must avoid uplifting any basic truths, such as the three sections of sanctification, the designation of Christ as the seed of David to be the first-born Son of God, the acknowledgment of the fact that "I am of Christ," etc., to cause divisions that divide Christ, including His Body (1 Cor. 1:11-13a). Some said that they belonged to Paul, some to Cephas, some to Apollos, and some, the

If we pick up sth narrow and hold on to it. as "we are of Christ."
"superior than anyone else", then it leads to division.
BE RIGHT IN FOLLOWING OTHERS　　　　63

"superior" ones, to Christ. However, Christ is not divided. You must be careful. You may teach the right truths, but to stress any one too much may be the cause of a division.

The application of the divine truths must also avoid neglecting any subordinate truths or stressing any of them, which leads toward the direction of division that divides the Body of Christ. Both to stress and to neglect certain truths may cause division. When we met in Elden Hall, quite often Pentecostal people would come to us with speaking in tongues. The brothers would inquire of me about them, but I would indicate that there was no problem. We allowed them to speak in tongues because it is in the Bible. I have studied much concerning speaking in tongues. I learned that even before the New Testament age, people already spoke in tongues by the power of demons. A brother from Ghana told us that when he returned to his homeland, he saw the unbelievers there speaking in tongues by the demons. Some speaking in tongues is by the demons, while some, although very little, is by the Holy Spirit. The Pentecostals, however, do not discern this. Not only is some speaking in tongues by demons; some is merely by the human power to speak syllables. This is neither by the Holy Spirit nor by the evil spirit, but simply by men themselves. Certain ones put their hands on your head and teach you to turn your tongue and say "Praise Jesus" very quickly. As a result, some syllables come out, which they claim is speaking in tongues. I analyzed this very much. Then I found out that this was only nonsense syllables, not a genuine tongue.

T. Austin-Sparks was a spiritual giant. He was very high. He was a top writer concerning eternal life, and we may even say that the line of eternal life in Christian writings stopped after his death. Once I invited him to Taipei. He was very strong against tongue-speaking; he opposed it too much. The Pentecostal people, however, stress it too much. They make the tongue to be the whole body. They say that when they speak in tongues, they are happy. To be sure, speaking in nonsense syllables will make you happy and very relaxed. In my study of this, however, I found a good point: Their intention is to contact the Lord, and sometimes spontaneously they did

contact the Lord. We cannot deny this. From this I learned
that not all wrong teachings are heresies. Some wrong teachings are simply wrong teachings. Therefore, we have to be
careful.

FOLLOWING OTHERS ACCORDING TO
THE DIVINE TRUTH AND THE DIVINE VISION

Since I came to this country in 1962, I have seen and experienced many things. Because there are so many co-workers
in this area, I feel burdened to speak this word of love as a
warning to you. Beware of these four "gophers," and be careful about following others. Actually, we should not follow
anyone. Concerning following a person, the New Testament
only tells us that Paul said, "Be imitators of me, as I also am
of Christ" (1 Cor. 11:1). We follow someone because he has the
revelation of God, the vision of God. I admit and I am bold
to say that God brought me to Brother Nee. I followed him;
I admit it. People shamed me, saying, "You only speak the
things Watchman Nee teaches." I said, "That is right. That is
my glory, not my shame." I never met another Christian
preacher who knew the Bible in this way. No one but Watchman Nee ever told me what the vision of God is, so I learned
of him. Since coming to this country, I have always tried my
best to keep on the central lane of the divine revelation. At
times in my speaking I was a little careless, but after my
message was polished and I read it again, I changed some
of the things which I had said. I have been very careful in
putting out my writings. In actuality, our leading is not a
person but the divine truth, the divine vision.

In February 1986 we had an urgent elders' conference in
which I spoke of the new way. Because the Lord's recovery
had become dormant, I was like Gideon, sounding the
trumpet to collect a group of people to fight for the recovery.
I had no intention to force everyone to follow me in the same
way. I told them that they may not follow me, but they should
not oppose. The next summer I told the saints that our
leading actually is not a person, neither I nor Brother Nee,
but it is the Lord's revelation, the Lord's word. Therefore, we
have to discern very much concerning the matter of the truth.

Then we will not damage the Body, damage ourselves, or damage the one whom we follow.

You must never try to get people to follow you. That is the serpent. It does not help you; it damages you. This also means that you should never follow any person; simply follow the Lord according to His Word and follow the heavenly vision. To this end, you must study His Word properly, without twisting or any kind of deforming. The full-time trainees must not say that they have come here to follow someone. They have come here to learn how to follow the Lord and to learn His Word in the proper way so that they can discern what are the basic truths and what are the subordinate truths. Some truths are like the trunk of a tree, and some truths are subordinate, like the branches. Moreover, some branches are bigger, while some are smaller. To understand and to accept the basic truths should be governed by God's economy, by Christ, and by His Body. Concerning the subordinate truths, the branches, do not oppose, neglect, or stress any one in particular.

A TESTIMONY CONCERNING
THE WAY TO FOLLOW OTHERS

I was together with Brother Nee for eighteen years. For eighteen years I never invited him to eat with me. Similarly, in our whole life together, Brother Nee invited me to his house only once; that was in 1948 when I stayed in his home in Foochow as his guest for one or two weeks. At that time, he invited me to a certain eating place where we could observe the eating habits of the Fukienese, but while we were together, we simply ate and did not speak improperly. In contrast, a certain brother often used to bring his followers to a coffee shop to drink together and speak in an improper way. I warned him about this. We must not have intimacy or friendship. Intimacy is not lovely; intimacy in the typology of the Bible is honey. In the meal offering honey was prohibited. The people could not put honey in the meal offering. Instead, they put in salt, which kills germs (Lev. 2:11, 13). We either do not love each other or we love by our natural life, which is honey. This corrupts us. I also believe that I never gave Brother Nee a gift. He only gave me two sets of books, Darby's

Synopsis of the Books of the Bible in five volumes and Dean Alford's *Greek New Testament*. He gave these to me in 1933, and they helped me very much. That was his shepherding and perfecting of me.

I am simply opening a small window to show you what kind of person Brother Nee was. We never joked together. At most, he once said that a certain brother, who was always in his mind and never in his spirit, may have been "saved but not regenerated." Among the saints, there are persons who seem to have a mind but no spirit. They know their mind, but they do not know their spirit. It is as if they have been redeemed judicially but not regenerated organically. Of course, this is not an actual fact, but there is this kind of person. This was Brother Nee's meaning.

Prayer: Lord, in spite of all these defects and mistakes made by us, we are not disheartened, discouraged, or disappointed. Rather, Lord, we are very much encouraged by You, by what You are, by what You have done, and by what You are still doing. Thank You, Lord, that You are still moving among us throughout the globe. We look unto You for further mercy and further grace. We look to You for further experience of You in our spirit to be our abiding grace. Oh, "the Lord be with your spirit. Grace be with you." We love this word of encouragement. Lord, we have no trust in our self. We are finished with our self-trusting. We trust in You. Lord, do saturate us and soak us to be everything within us, to be our faith, our joy, our peace, our rest, and our comfort. Thank You that You are our Shepherd without, and You are our Comforter as the life-giving Spirit within. We trust in You for Your recovery, for Your move. Lord, remember each one of us. We are on Your heart, and we are even on Your breast. Lord, never forget us. We thank You that You will never forget us. We are really on Your heart. Thank You, Lord, for Your mercy to have all the churches in Southern California. Lord, bless all the saints. Bless Your recovery. Bless all the churches. Bless all of our service in the one work for Your unique recovery. Amen.

Be right in following others:

1. Be careful in following any co-workers whom you appreciate and to whom you are attracted:
   a. He should be a person loving the Lord, living for the Lord, and renouncing his self, natural life, preference, and ambition.
   b. He must hold the complete revelation of the entire holy Scriptures properly without any twisting and deforming.
   c. He must be one who endeavors to keep the oneness of the Spirit, the oneness of the universal Body, by taking the unique ground of the local church.
2. Be strongly discerning in the accepting of the divine revelation according to the holy Scriptures:
   a. The accepting of the divine revelation must be governed by:
      1) The eternal economy of God as the basic principle.
      2) Christ as the centrality and universality of God's eternal economy.
      3) The Body of Christ which consummates the New Jerusalem as the divine goal of the processed and consummated Triune God.
   b. The application of the divine truths must avoid: *Economy Christ Life*
      1) Uplifting any basic truths, such as the three sections of sanctification, the designation of Christ as the seed of David to be the firstborn Son of God, the acknowledgment of the fact that "I am of Christ," etc., to cause divisions that divide Christ, including His Body (1 Cor. 1:11-13a).
      2) Neglecting any subordinate truths or stressing any of them, which leads toward the direction of division that divides the Body of Christ.

A facsimile of the placard prepared by Brother Lee
for the co-workers who heard his word of love. Brother Lee
advised the co-workers to place it in a visible location
and read it every day for a month.

ABOUT THE AUTHOR

Witness Lee was born in 1905 in northern China and raised in a Christian family. At age 19 he was fully captured for Christ and immediately consecrated himself to preach the gospel for the rest of his life. Early in his service, he met Watchman Nee, a renowned preacher, teacher, and writer. Witness Lee labored together with Watchman Nee under his direction. In 1934 Watchman Nee entrusted Witness Lee with the responsibility for his publication operation, called the Shanghai Gospel Bookroom.

Prior to the Communist takeover in 1949, Witness Lee was sent by Watchman Nee and his other co-workers to Taiwan to ensure that the things delivered to them by the Lord would not be lost. Watchman Nee instructed Witness Lee to continue the former's publishing operation abroad as the Taiwan Gospel Bookroom, which has been publicly recognized as the publisher of Watchman Nee's works outside China. Witness Lee's work in Taiwan manifested the Lord's abundant blessing. From a mere 350 believers, newly fled from the mainland, the churches in Taiwan grew to 20,000 in five years.

In 1962 Witness Lee felt led of the Lord to come to the United States, and he began to minister in Los Angeles. During his 35 years of service in the U.S., he ministered in weekly meetings and weekend conferences, delivering several thousand spoken messages. Much of his speaking has since been published as over 400 titles. Many of these have been translated into over fourteen languages. He gave his last public conference in February 1997 at the age of 91.

He leaves behind a prolific presentation of the truth in the Bible. His major work, *Life-study of the Bible,* comprises over 25,000 pages of commentary on every book of the Bible from the perspective of the believers' enjoyment and experience of God's divine life in Christ through the Holy Spirit. Witness Lee was the chief editor of a new translation of the New Testament into Chinese called the Recovery Version and directed the translation of the same into English. The Recovery Version also appears in a number of other languages. He provided an extensive body of footnotes, outlines, and spiritual cross references. A radio broadcast of his messages can be heard on Christian radio stations in the United States. In 1965 Witness Lee founded Living Stream Ministry, a non-profit corporation, located in Anaheim, California, which officially presents his and Watchman Nee's ministry.

Witness Lee's ministry emphasizes the experience of Christ as life and the practical oneness of the believers as the Body of Christ. Stressing the importance of attending to both these matters, he led the churches under his care to grow in Christian life and function. He was unbending in his conviction that God's goal is not narrow sectarianism but the Body of Christ. In time, believers began to meet simply as the church in their localities in response to this conviction. In recent years a number of new churches have been raised up in Russia and in many European countries.

OTHER BOOKS PUBLISHED BY
Living Stream Ministry

Titles by Witness Lee:

Titles by Watchman Nee:

Available at
Christian bookstores, or contact Living Stream Ministry
2431 W. La Palma Ave. • Anaheim, CA 92801
1-800-549-5164 • www.livingstream.com